MW01687819

night flying

for Leonor :)

night flying

~~Laurie Anne Fuhr~~

Laurie Fuhr

Thank you for your kind ongoing support as a poet of Poetry Café! I love hearing your poems.

♡ LF
xo 2020

Frontenac House Poetry

Book design: Neil Petrunia, Epix Design
Cover Image: Kelly Sutherland
Author photo: Miranda Krogstad

Library and Archives Canada Cataloguing in Publication

Fuhr, Laurie, author
Night flying / Laurie Anne Fuhr.

Poems.
Issued in print and electronic formats.
ISBN 978-1-927823-82-8 (softcover).--ISBN 978-1-927823-91-0 (PDF)

I. Title.

PS8561.U454N54 2018 C811'.6 C2018-903934-5
C2018-903935-3

Frontenac House gratefully acknowledges the support of the Canada Council for the Arts for our publishing program. We would also like to thank the Government of Alberta Multimedia Development Fund for their support of our publishing program.

Canada Council for the Arts Conseil des Arts du Canada Alberta Government

Printed and bound in Canada
Published by Frontenac House Ltd.
1648 Bowness Road NW
Calgary, Alberta, T2N 3J9, Canada
Tel: 403-263-7025

frontenachouse.com

Contents

For military brats everywhere.

night flying

The up-there
shredded, hanging
in flystrip with our nerves

stuck on it. Screw us,
we're in turnaround
airspace.

~ Karen Solie,
"Air Show"
Pigeon

night flying

clear afternoon sound at night, clocks
start running backwards   hands
sucked counterclockwise break
from the face, get pulled
through engines   small birds fly
into the earth, feather-stripped
by g-force windshear

F-18 roar is short low rumble then sure
long growl, all action, no
foreplay   rabid machine
gone cannibalistic, eating the sky
it's made of, transforms
into what it consumes

houses shake, their occupants take too far
their refusal to be stirred, grow
stagnant   playground bolts
knock loose, dooming children
to a fate not bad as bullies
imitating daddies   clouds
are vacuumed, spat clear

to Primrose Lake, raining carcasses
of fish-turned-fishiles splashed onshore
by missile tests   armchair golfers
in rec room dark taste divot dirt
at the first subsonic
warning   trained ears turn it
to concentrated silence

as a barrel roll overhead
rolls up, wrings out, sprays the base
with all associations:

sudden storms   the hurricane
they didn't hear coming   terrorists
known histories of airshow
accidents   freak crashes

unimportant moments
plowed deep into memory

when a pilot flies too far
from the sun, breaks
the sound barrier   sonic
boom   reverse-Icarus
falls off into a lake
of sky

applicable skills of the military brat #1

as an adult, you'll have trouble painting or making holes in walls.
your blank white house will be bare as a bunker, will smell
of plastic-wrapped bar soap, Ivory or Lux. for now,

Mom lets you choose one full-sized poster from the CanEx each year.
Lady and the Tramp means a year of asking for spaghetti;

grown up, it means dollar store candles in pot-metal holders
and cravings for slender men with terrier beards, bookish sociopaths
for whom love is not a catalyst, is fact estranged from impact.

for now, don't worry. insist on a world of cauterizing sweetness.
smile like a rabbit, bite your bottom lip, make farting sounds

at the sleep-over party, tape and recite weird British commercials
for your friends. being laughed at is better than being ignored;
shame, an emotion yet to be learned. work with it.

F-18 cycle

Dads give out DND trading cards for death machinery
with missiles not hockey sticks, a glaring absence of pink gum

but when it sits in the book next to Gretzky and Lemieux,
the hope / dream / hunger for future gets transferred "how 'bout

them Hornets" little soldier marches off to school, brown-bag
rations in hand, pent-up explosions for gym period floor hockey

bullied

my brother clenches his stomach
like a pilot in tailspin,

like Dad said to try
on roller coasters,

keep falling-sickness
under control.

it never works.

melancholia

sunlight through smoke-yellow drapes
is chloroform, special occasion jewelry
little anchors to drag her down.

queen mattress frothed in bedskirt
produces undertow.

after school in Germany
we find her drowning in bed,
feed her air from a paper bag.

long red hair fanned upward like a diver's,
panic lowers her down
without a bell,

hydrophobe dreaming front crawl
how others dream flight.

dirt fills ears like water,
fear resounds through deep earth.

a bedroom is a natural subwoofer,
its reverb chamber
drums rudiments to hell.

death hears Dad
come home early,

turns its ready ghosts away.

applicable skills of the military brat #2

today you fold your life under cardboard flaps.
divorce the privacy of Private Married Quarters.

meet an overseas moving truck the size of a continent.
smell diesel cologne on the men loading boxes.

feel how cold a place seems without curtains.
save your best things like the house was on fire.

watch Dad move, a fleet changing course.
hear his rivets creak under strain.

say goodbye to all your friends.
climb your favourite tree.

there is no way to know
how leaving will feel later.

track your course with caution:
a contrail can't lead you home.

leaving Germany

for Mom

an empty PMQ between packing and leaving
is grave silent, thunderous when boxes are gone.

preparing the apartment for final inspection,
the amplified slap of Mom's slippers
on government-issued linoleum
excites and hushes us.

polyester pantlegs schlep by.
I reach for her,

my small skull a barrier
between her echoing chest
and the empty apartment.

the last mirror severed from its dresser
stares into us. we close eyes,
brace against hollowness,

our still reflections
ready to be packed.

Alberta winter gothic

The lake

Will not apologize for what he's stolen,
for what he's eaten then spit up on the shore.

~ Micheline Maylor,
"The lake"
Full Depth: The Raymond Knister Poems

Alberta winter gothic

we walk the milk-draped provincial park,
birch bark wind-peeled in transparent strips reveals
a trace vein of every missing leaf   my boots
trailblaze deep for your shoes, prints warm your feet

watch silent as disaster surveyors the broken-tree
sculptures   one, a boat, builds itself out to dock
with a sky turned bluer steel than snow for eyes
in it long enough, shade of lake ice scraped clean

to the drifted-in amphitheatre, breaker ship cutting the park.
capacity-audience of bench snowpiles captive til thaw
knees me deep in stage. you listen to my memory poem,
think how it isn't for you like so much else

while we gaze long darkening treelines for creature-
hunger sensed there. but the French boy who lurks
in his poem stealthy as a deer   heavy as a bear
steps further into the bush. on entering your ears

my words and I only ever been yours.

turn your head like a birch

green eyes rustle skin
like asking, like yes.
turn your head like a birch,

map acoustic geography
up outstretched arms to ears.
turn your head like a birch

how arms reach, dark jacket
on white forest,
colours numb as hands.

nine month winter as poison gas

North Alberta night is made up
of goosehonk and coyote yelp.
pain tangos with wolves, hackled,
weird music of frozen leaves in wind.

oaks, being louder, hurt more than pines
but pines send all sound
down raggedy branches to harm you
through a sill's cracked defenses.

wombful of papery foliage
needs birth, but aurora
juts through eyes
up from boreal stomach
in a sneak attack of burrowing season.

nine month winter is poison gas,
air too cold to breathe.
in weakest freeze,
our handbuilt shelter

suffers crude road-crew burial
spread-eagled in drift,
shock gelled to stuck lens,
permanent snow angels—

death refracts forever
in immortal molecules,
hydrogen-two-oxygen
of snowflake, liquid, and lifting gas.

hero(i)n(e)

he couldn't believe me about herons unnamed
in the café coffee table book: one Great Grey

one Great Blue searched each page
for labeled ones speculated
each long-necked wrong-coloured bird
could be the same. what does it mean
he can't trust me about

birds, can't trust me about
beauty, my own he says is there
that without label I can't name
and disbelieve him,

riffle through books for my long neck,
my beak, needing to know what I'm called—
but books are mirrors and magazines,
my GreatGreyGreatBlue eyes aren't there,

I fly different. pictures in a book don't do
justice, he prefers his herons, his heroines
more fabulous how close up in person

at Wakaw Lake, one Blue sighting per lifetime
is handfuls of feathers brushed across your palm
when you point its trail across the sky,
when air softens with point of view confusion,
special effects through regular lens,

breeze of their flight lifts tiny hairs
on the back of my hand

so fingers ride enigma wingman,
delicate shotgun.

dead reckoning

if piano had a human voice it would be Carole King.

half a verse away from a sad song, prairie sky
a high-traffic area for East-going storms
on a jetstream Yellowhead, I lie on ears

blued with jazz, turn off eyes like a house to sleep.
closed, they adjust to mind dark
until they see a second room,
white reverse-silhouettes,

photo negatives developing thoughts as they form.

to source reflections on the rain-soaked streets
of a nighttime mind is to feel too mortal,
taste the marrow in your bones.

dawn fog on half a window censors roofs and trees,

skies it all to grey-green treetops
faint through mist tissue, half a tornado warning,
clear light blue calm above.

get out of bed on faith the day will provide reasons for living.

think abolished 'gender differences in navigation
strategies,' landmark slash compass orientation,
ie. anything goes. try measuring devices

for subjective time: the speed of confectionary coffee
(before it cools) sets a pace to minimize
morning slippage, lessen lost-time accidents.

no longer in the running for experience, what raced them there?

third person one of the many she employs for distance
in a land with no borders, no maps or trail guide
but imaginary lines connect symbols dredged

from thin air, form loose astral countries,
constellations for primitive course-plotting:
piano-to-house-to-street-to-storm

and back again to bed.

waiting bubbles

set down the small crystal bowl
of chocolate caramel ice cream
and spoon handle clinks bell edge high E
of the work phone ring, wrong
number voice in her ear again,
right ear they say listens closer to music—
wasn't the caller's fault
he wasn't him she waited for
when she turned the knob

on the espresso machine,
withstood long steamings,
beading bulletproof mascara,
hated little bubbles she made
full of milk and waiting
that pop so easy, mock her
with dance, organize their chaos,
pointless as the sense
of waiting   unbearable loud shoosh

of steam in a tin pitcher as waiting
deafens her ears from a chance
to answer a call, eyes stuck on
the thermoguage slide up to red
a similar crescent arc
to opening door, red at its height
the moment of seeing who—
finger burnt waiting, she didn't

feel the talk button depress
under her tip-seared index
when she answered the wrong number,
                                        wrong hope

hung up without
even saying

field recording

poem beginning with a line by Carolyn Forché

as the fence has recorded the wind,
so the fence's wood has played it back,
sung watery ripples
from eyes like pursed mouths
a music only heard in the body.

it gets there how prairie wind
burrows through jackets,
layers of cotton-blend skin.

field music overfills flesh,
overflows underneath
to trip other senses.

North wind flows inside
to lodge winter there
before it even hits the ground.

snow-white scleras
should have given it away
but the mirror's silver
burnished them to fool me

how grey grass poking out of snow
sterlings a whole scene.

finally, the fence's weathered wood
of stored-up summer
thaws the song.

in January, the sudden flavour
of dandelion milk
in my mouth.

walking home

crunch of birch strips in my pocket,
supplies for an imaginary basket.

how brittle and see-through
are what are not your fingers

when woven instead
to scraps of alone

posting: Ottawa (1994-1999)

everybody leaves a mark
somehow
you have to know how to look

~ rob mclennan
"he says a name for water"
bagne, or Criteria for Heaven

lithology

have entered into land
without shadows.
interior city in even greylight
casts nothing, won't try
to emphasize or catch.
all of us equally plain now
in colourstripped clothes, sallowed skin.

strange, jagged tulips come up late
by the old Terry Fox bridge.
pumped northward through pipeline
tulip stems into the cup
we're poured & out.
concrete skin / flesh sidewalk
are samed by their ugliness.

the red oil in tulip blooms
won't dye what it holds
but paints us darker in the quick soak
by comparison   colour applied
gone immediately black, oxidized
in the inside-out oxygen molecule
of an overcast morning after.

crazy annie

I spoke to this woman,
the movements of fish made her hungry.
she wanted to fill her mouth with that grace,
taste the sudden motions of its flowing
swim   tongue the beady roundness
of its eyes   trace along gill until
relative chin. she wanted to become the fish,
swallow whole, install its soul
then fillet, whole body
dropped away from the scaly gold float,
from greasy opalescence
of seashell on velvet fish pictures
in Vietnamese Pho noodlehouses.

outside the National Gallery

I

because we look through your tinted sunroof
the sky turns around itself clouds inside-
out their shadows surface

sky brown-green
colour of tornadoes   wind in vertical flags
sounds drama classroom thunder. we climb
the tank

embrace stillness   silent storm
descends dark, lowers readymade thunder—
silver-spired cathedral / stone buildings / concrete
wind, your black coat against it all solid
unmoving, me hanging on molds you an anchor
this boat above roiling sea below pavement
sky flagpoles and flags: masts and sails: cars
float by—

II

your black coat against it all solid unmoving:
carves you statue shapes me sculptor / tank
a headstone, masts gate sentinels (cathedral doors
St. Peter waiting) / storm-sky hell or limbo / wind
urging decision
(afterall for us to make

III   your
black wool coat against it all solid, you
unmoving in dreamscape, shifting with lava
cloudfloes in wind / cathedral spires erupting through
their silver / window fissures / pavement: techtonic,
cooled sky / this country the island spread out from it /
flagpoles: tallships buried (evidence: water once) /
sky billows smoke and ash not ready (yet) to rain
but rising pressure felt in ears / pounded out by churchbells
ringing six o' clock / time forms real /
bells ring us back to real /

IV   we drive away
your red car   you   your black coat against it all
the one solid thing kept you real / holding on to you
kept me corporeal kept the world from splitting up
into storm / ocean / heaven / hell /
cemetery / volcano / apocalypse

V
peaceful, we, against it all

                          on a tank
                                    our cannon pointed
all potential targets :silent open mouth
waiting for the kiss

that later
          (in your new apartment)
won't go off

                          [last second sensing
danger (a cannon could fire any moment,
could explode)].

coupon

for Pat

an e unloops as daisy petals
in too-humid summer,
upswept e's of sunwriting
cross a blankspace (any such
not left alone), graffito
cloudwisps across a burning
sky inky-bluebell colour
donated by treestumps.
muddy shade, moist
moss, spring beebumble
further into the glade where
our picnic misses a canopener,
edges of checkers
not sharp enough

so you with a stick
guage your inner Boy Scout
against factory (man) and
alum (nature) under god (dammit)
all odds against you now
licking beanjuice off your
fingers (the ants feast
a month or more, their
rank numbers unrolling dotted-
lines to cut along
a coupon of time to 'clip
and save' in a scrapbook
beside pressed leaves
that are scrapbooks themselves,
autumn stamped into them
& summer too, the opposite
page)

absolutely Lebreton Street

for David S.

mobiles made of typewriter parts
clack the air in sway.
the words I need hang there.
2 years, you say, *to build that.*
I don't tell you *by now*
you could have written
a novel. I'll tell the novelist
by now you could have built
a mobile. anyway,
you're a better authority on now
than I am, here in your house
where there's plenty of furniture
strewn around
but nothing to say
that won't incriminate me,
nothing to say that will.

beers with the King of Shillington

for Jay

the voice is becoming sound.
the ear is becoming listen.
the mouth is becoming,
he tells me, while his becomes
half gone, parts gin
to tonic & apple juice.

Jay's left sideburn, higher
than the other, belies a secret desire
to climb a hill one side
at a time, beginning
with his left leg.

sly smile in the left radio,
the o's open end projects this
as sound that slides from
the cursive top hornmouth of its
vowel
becomes mouth,
listen
becomes ear &
sound
becomes voice,

he tells with his, half full
still ignobly, insolently uneven.
hey you! roll down the hill,
be your best Jill.
convenient edit, the part where
she overtakes & runs him down.

your crown must needs
replacing, my friend.
we have several safe alternatives
in unordinary household items:
chain link, pheasant feathers,
crooked antlers from an unknown beast
suit you better. you are hereby ordained

King of Shillington Avenue, adorned
by your own weird decor.
the West End is your kingdom:
rule cruelly with a cotton thumb
so the fist can never go iron.

stopping time

for Craig S.

4 a.m. Chase Diner.
time stops by careful placement
of televisions, windows,
mirrors. a mirror
is as many images
as there are points of view,

as many people drinking
bad coffee eating
all night breakfasts with
all day breakfast sausages
left over, as many sausages

as there are surfaces to
reflect them, upside-down
sausages produced
in the factory-curve
of stainless spoons,
links linked by industrial shine
of water-spotted knives.

minutes are consumed
with each bite of syrup-soaked toast,
every piece of pancake sponged full
then poured again
from the slow decanter,
second by second, minutes,
hours absorbed with French toast.

pendulum stops with a bite
of the egg clock, yolk face.
pepper speckles abacus
moments, enumerate, account.

we cycle the room, our hands spin
on arms like Mickey Mouse's,
our eyes rise & set,
suns and moons, gold-plated,

our hearts spin,

knobs that wind
& release us same time.

a face is a picture more often than a face

for rob

a face is a picture more often than a face,
a body a sweater, a mouth a moustache.
voice long as highways opens street names,
words of poems I once heard you say.

traffic circles deepen as cars go by,
a bio-erosion mistaken for aging.
the window you're framed behind preserves:
enough MSG, Chinese lanterns can't get you.

time is linear so poets can't follow.
my heart turns 16 again   your liver turns 60.
a picture turns into a face, a sweater into warm.
fear of not writing again turns into a poem.

never knew where I was until I left a place,
new air blued my lungs, acclimatized marrow.
where airplanes set you down, you're home.
wherever you are is nowhere that left me.

framing Riopelle

two weeks before he died, one
week before I was dead to you,
Madame's giant Riopelle lay
on the floor of Market gallery,
black splotches the close-up
of a gnat landing pad.

I help you frame it,
hold down corners
as you held me down
through my own hands.
I am a flea on the painting of your life,
tiny fly trapped in the frame.

maybe we killed Jean-Paul,
he couldn't breathe behind
all that museum glass we cased him in—
I couldn't breathe there either.

glossproof detours the welcome glare,
blinds out part of the total picture,
plasticizes the natural scene.
lets the specimen fly away
from a cage of woven light,

dripping ink that turns
to shadow on contact.

rules for combustion

for Cara

tonight his mood is black.
the fire won't start for us.
speech leaves him, eye contact
becomes impossible.

coming home, the road is a snake,
downcurves harbour
bottomless shadows, waxing moon
lights the hills: a pinspot.

his back aches from shouldering
snow he moved; what he lifted
weighed him, but what presses down
is fresh heaviness.

at home, cats keep vigil
over the smallest noises of the night
beside weak fire. kindling
refuses to be its name.

once, flames caught so easily
we'd begin to blaze across
an empty bar. heat between us
was enough to warm a room.

do we need more fuel?
more air?
has our composition changed?
the environment become inhospitable?

after suffering a long chill,
Cara takes time to kneel,
put on gloves, add wood to the stove,
blow on embers.

we wake in the night
warmed by her perseverance,
her faith, conditions we lack
burning away the cold in us.

in which C is absorbed by an alleyway

tonight I realized
the stoop in the top of your posture
is every time you bent to hold her.
you reached out so often
it broke you.

smoking in the alleyway,
your shadow shadows
by a row of streetlights.
each blurry replica
represents a year to come.

they hunch off
unto the ages, get
progressively smaller.

as with love,
the easy weight of an 80 watt bulb
gets heavier the longer you hold it.

at the end of the line
your last shadow shrinks off,
fades into blackness around.

pavement ends

There is a tomorrow in which
I drift into the sky, and the earth
becomes a wee dot, so tiny
it disappears, and you are on it
so you vanish too.

~ Stuart Ross,
"I Left My Heart In"
I Cut My Finger

'people live here for the quiet'

for Dad

down- and up- trail behind
the house back fences, ATVs rip
the strip from the trail's beginning
tab says *pull*, and they're off,
sonic peal peels yards
away from tranquil forest.

eleven-thirty Saturday,
cars pick calmest streets to blast
with gas through piston
to pure rev and squeal, gutters
stretching off front lawn edges
like gum from a shoe,
pavement melted.

coyotes playing hyena
yelp quick crazed yelps,
pass night through nostril flare,
bloody fresh-kill throats pump lungs
until fur is a stand of exclamation marks
in a forest of calm punctuation.

airframes chomp / devour / digest air so quickly
each oxygen molecule spins top-like,
sharpens to puncture a tiny void
in the space it once held,
making way for vapour trails
in the anaerobic sky.

Dad gets the plastic string
of his Father's Day Weed Wacker
rightway, ruthlessly thrusts
the enormous amorous drone
of a ten-foot round bee
in all the lawn's secret places,

then the leaf blower:
constant Airbus toilet flush
drops its unthinkable contents
over the countryside,
scatologics of sound ick
landing over Cold Lake North.

the grin behind the screen door yells
"this baby's got some power, eh?!",
same face said it came for the peace,
stayed for the quiet,

same lips smiled this grown face
much smaller then,

same voice that throat
oh loud-kid glee!

routine 2 – summer

Sunday on-Base, fabric-softener haze softens
the cedar trees, our dads turn into each other
trying to be Eastwood in civvies,
The Duke in a ball cap.

the smell at five, first propane then
barbecuing meat, one big outdoor kitchen
your nose leads you home through,
hungry for what your neighbour has
and for chicken legs blackened on Dad's grill.

children trying to be different from parents
trying to be the same end up duplicates,
walk in and out of identical dwellings
until parents forget how many children they have,
feed them all just to be safe.

carbon-copy suns sink through identical
stormdoor windows, the Canadian Military
syncs eleven o'clock bedtime insides
with the knob that turns down gas on the grill,

turns their own fires clockwise,
Westerly, faces burning towards Monday war games
and the crisp uniform edge of Canada.

Saskatchewan

low skies going grey
with the age of rain.
wisdom of wind-swept canola, bright
broken pickets by the crossing, dark
the lines that count days
in a cell.

red steel conduit
carries the train current,
old black cars with handwritten
Canadian Pacific half-rubbed
away   train itself half-rubbed away:
electricity fading.

soon to disappear with grain elevators
and my grandfather's cabin.

a storm moves in and out again.
every time I say goodbye
it rains, I never judge how much
or little, couldn't say how you fell.

powerlines bridge the air, I walk across
with eyes balancing sight, fall
into hayfields turned to heather.
lie awhile in the ether,
watch clouds roll childlike:

never telling their years old
on frail fingers of light.

prairie cryptic

combines in the dark
could be harvesting anything

hummingbird clouds: a cycle

everything darkens under thundercloud shadows
but the canola fields, yielding unrefined light. 𝄋
this is where hummingbirds go in August

when they disappear from gardens to fields
like moth cocoon night to a day of flame,
burning in tractor gas red blue and green.

tiny pyros self-immolate, flit
across prairies, set them on fire.
smoke rises from crops, becomes low-hanging cloud.

everything darkens under thundercloud shadows
but the canola fields, yielding unrefined light.
D.S. al Coda.

mud pie

for Jeff

Wakaw Lake Saskatoonberry pie tastes best
after a swim in Wakaw Lake, is best served
with Wakaw lakewater up your nose,
unfamous Wakaw Lake mud oozing
between toes. townspeople say
the mud has healing powers,
a rural myth   a way to forgive it
for stinking up swimsuits.
rocks, rotmulched weeds
and the bones of dead perch

make a cast of each foot 'til
you lift it   we imagine
foreign objects in muck
into fossils, prehistoric evidence left behind
by the glacier that carved Wakaw
Lake   and Wakaw Saskatoonberries
fed in fossil soil mean
next bite of pie could feed you
fleeting-image insights,

your prehistoric tongue
long in taste as a brontosaur's
picking up subtle far-off flavours:
salt of the ocean the glacier crossed
to get here, yellow shock
of Ontario bee pollen dancing coordinates
of sweet maple Quebec,
arrowhead silt of Manitoba rivers
and wildflower wheat
cultivated by swathing winds,
eventual breezes confounding the surface
of Wakaw Lake.

the man of words

in memory of Grandpa Fuhr

the man of words can tell you
the slight ways clouds change rolling over Saskatoon,
bloom out in branches above tree-lines,
up like castles over the Bessborough.

the man of words has news about
stock markets, who's in Parliament,
hockey scores, lotto numbers,
the Royal Family.

the man of words gives you too much info,
hears birds when he talks, greets them over
and over, sings vowels, crowds the air
with his sounds.

but the man of few words speaks
with the curve of his shoulders
and the straight of his posture, listens
with the shadows in his ears, holds

honesty in his hands' curve,
their placement on the dinner table.
the small smile on his lips
says all you need to know.

golfing in heaven

for Walter and Diana

I
named for a forest goddess,
your father a minister,
you're religious and mythical,
ancient, primeval.

at the reception, you tell of miracles
that happen without notice,
of the farmer who found Dad in a ditch
on Mother's Day,

of Dad on the phone
saying "It's okay, Mom,"
though they said he was comatose,
near-death-experienced.

did he close his eyes on cold glow
of windshield stars, open them
on dark prairie night and bastard new moon,
anaemic moon, greenish-glow moon?

thinking, before pain set in,
he'd traveled in his dreams?

since Grandpa died last Monday
Dad's back in the ditch, waiting for help,
eyes open, pain rushing by
at the speed of hydro poles,

too fast for his mind
to catch up.

II
for years of visits to Saskatoon after,
Dad disappears before we're awake
to have Timmy's with Grandpa,
read the paper together.

his place of faith
an address I can't get to,
knowing nowhere other than
where all of me is,

yet the claustrophobia of hell
is portable and compact,
compatible with nothingness.

III
I hand my brother
a floppy cushion, say
it's a funeral home,
you'd figure they could stuff things better

and my joke isn't funny, Jeff gets mad
but I am angrier, livid at the death staff
that didn't make Grandpa
look like he was sleeping

but like the sad, dead thing
that made my father sob
the first time I
heard him cry.

Dad stands in the flower-fragrant apartment
days before, humid with his mother's tears,
grief's greenhouse conditions,

decades of suits stand on their hangers
without a man inside,
a wardrobe of Grandpa missing.

III

on the eternal golf course,
Grandpa's pastel polo shirt
and tan shorts, tan skin,

gold cross with bling chain flashing,
well-sunned, relaxed, and amused,
making small-town Saskatchewan
a little Hawaii, summer as any resort.

applying night cream, Granny tells me
When I can't sleep, I go golfing
with Grandpa in Wakaw.
I'm always asleep by the third hole.

when I can't sleep,
let me caddy.

vanishing point

You still hear people say, "Well there is nothing to look at in the prairie." I mean, that just makes me furious! Every mile is different.

~ Robert Kroetsch,
Video interview – Lieutenant Governor of Alberta Distinguished Artist Awards, 2011

vanishing point

hydro poles wait in line by the highwayside
for a chance to stare at your car, grubby-cheeked
with the false innocence of children expecting candy
hurled from a German Fasching parade float.
they watch the solo procession pass,

rumours in a code of long-distance-
conversational-lingo, words plucked as notes
from the three-string fretless bass
of their stretching, soundhole sky.
Blake's bass missing a string, fingers played
more quickly to compensate

as when he broke a taut stress-length of me,
made music from what was left
then drove away into dropped-D mountains
alone. perpetual Crowsnest landslide

buries notebooks, cursive script of tourist lit,
rewrites paper daydreams of mutual escape,
even Calgary too much like the world of men.
that he doesn't call breaks the roots and fives
of electric crosses, leaves them quiet
without his voice's amplifying current

so even blue fields of snow prairie
won't bloom, crops of white neon vibrate
grey-purple sky, melt barn rooves.
out from the biggest stable, electric crosses
march like soldiers into forever, airborne shuffle

through cramped deployment hatch of vanishing point
to usher one another without parachute
but with billowing canvas sky packed by atmosphere.
cord cut they drift free, make airfoil of strings and twigs
from small brown beaks who, mid-build,

line the homely sky, net it, make of its weavework
a giant chute designed to slow
the world at the end of its drag race, at its end
with the sleek comets of space-time.
ozone holes in engine leak fuel so black

headlights glance off the silver coating of ice stars,
eyeblink on Highway 2 when you think
you see lightning   car muffles winter,
thunder stalls the heavy hollow thud-crashes
of caskets falling from cranes, winter storm sound,

caskets made cylindrical
by the polishing wind of lightspeed descent,
ice stars' silver coating
little mirrors worn from the neck,
dog tags on electric crosses
that arrive at the front lines

of some senseless war over the country
at the edge of the earth, scream
the ultrasonic protest song, click of snow crust crystals
quake across fields how buzz leaps
on word-filled wires of electric crosses,
forced to carry themselves as they pass

on the road to self-crucifixion,
boughs of roadkill antlers laid in their path
palm fronds or poles of cedar, biblical,
world tree of Ezekiel ending empires,
reverberations, poor reception
beds voices in cracklines

and curved eyecorners of woodknot
stored for chants of later ceremony
when electric crosses resurrect from sloughs
by their own holiness
and strength of drivers' visual hope,
eyestrain for their image the thin-lidded prayer

to see them hike, arms out for balance
in the rough terrain and steady upward climb
of smooth-and-flat-everlasting, prepared for the moment
the vanishing point's portable hole swallows them
into Alice's tract, when grown she becomes a house

and the extra-dimensional driveway runs
into her apron. electric crosses kid themselves
that their arms could stop descent, make it quicker
to reach for guns when no smooth Swiss movement
could save that watch, no hands ending arms

it slips off, lost in the snowbank
while your car hustles electric crosses,
rustles cattle toward the doom
of black market butchery, dark phlebotomy
that ends the last drive trail,
bells of ice around necks refuse to chime

and lo too low to hear
except in the bottom hum of expansive
communication, as much a miracle across landspan
as over water, frosted sea bed
churns out small 4-legged animals,
gophers, rabbits, like sped-up

evolution   hare's ears keep record
of eras skipped as they hop the direction
electric crosses travel, hurled spears
wake upright from the sides
of grazing absent buffalo,
arrowheads uproot to throw themselves

at the red bullseye that bleats
on the deserving Colonial target
to win back the unceded countryside,
rightfully burn the wooden settlements
as threshers harvest rubble mills

and fur-trading huts, ghosts wear
coonskin caps, raccoon ghosts
keep spectral heads warm,
forefathers shake fat fists
while combines plow all of this
into grain, so bread that tastes of earth and sun

tastes also of sorrow and progress
in a piece of toast chewed down quickly
before he gets in a car that stalls on highways
and points its long station wagon hood,
sideview wings too small for flight

like those of an electric cross, drives towards forever
completely oblivious   (dashboard lit interior
insinuating dim mind mood)   just what, by symbol
of electricity   power pole   God   dead empire
he was getting himself into.

unable to trust a woman, he trusts eternity
made singular, poked out before him
the furthest speck of sight the naked eye can see
that never gets closer or further, shuffles ahead,
stays in sight a concerned friend but
her back to him, too far away

to hear from or speak to without telephone,
to line up words single file towards it
inside high-spanning wires, crossed t's that trudge
like electric crosses away from history
and its terms including love and my name

into the pitiless, nameless exclamation point of forever
where the tall vertical of marvel
is how straight a woman stands
before she collapses

in the affirmative posture
of electric crosses,
of brown jumpsuits that hurtle

to vanish in the endless freefall
of impossible dreams
and senseless oblivion

into the soft and endless,
into the patient waiting embrace
of sloughs.

posting: Winnipeg (1998-2001)

and this is it
how the world happens for me
this is the place
I am here
wherever I am I am
here

~ Patrick Friesen,
"easter"
Unearthly Horses

under pressure

for Mary Helen

I

as for the bouffant hairdos still practiced
in the beauty shops of the West,
the questionable masculinity of the ozone hole over Edmonton
and the extent
of known drift: chemicals skied, worn, or transported
in the pressurized containers of bodies

I can only tell you the label says *explosive*
the women must be hot, they take off their blouses
the blue edge, pursed tense
then asperitas clouds lapse:
rapidly undulating cartoon labia,
Pink Floyd-grotesque.

if butterfly wings cause storms—what, this, in Japan?
the PM won't declare a state of emergency—too male,
too Conservative.
Toronto upgrades Terror Threat Level to Yellow/Elevated—
fashion police are standing by.

II

Emergency Preparedness Canada warns, *Prepare for Tomorrow Today.*
I try but tomorrow turns into today and there's no siren.
7:30 in Newfoundland and the fish are finished dinner; in Alberta
they're just getting hungry. people are hungry all the time.

Ann-Marie at Tangles could tell you
breathing spray all day the back of your throat, sticky,
feels starved.

or Grandma Britton who owned
the Churchill Beauty Salon of Saskatoon,
did Joni Mitchell's mom's hair, six-degreeing us
to another's fortune greater than
our immediate-degree women will ever get but where is
a song for her, blue,
perm solution chemicals pressurized
the contained space of the basement salon,
of her lungs

the oxygen tank forty years too late
connected to her nose,
not a building's HVAC system.

food the only pleasure now, and only unpleasurable food.
her air supply won't fit the growing size of her body,
stupid doctor says go ahead with the open flame, it's too late,
let her keep smoking.

one day soon in Summerland seniors' apartment complex Winnipeg,
in whatever season

the perpetual summer sun of artificially lit atriums will explode,
University Crescent
light up the rest
of its moon a moment,
tear a new hole
in the feminine Manitoban sky,

blow off blouses along with their shadows
and every nearby 'do proximity-bouffed.

III
whoever or wherever you are, Alberta's coming for you.

          in L.A., Joni prepares to release an album of prairie-girl songs
she'll dedicate to her Little Green, the daughter she gave up
for adoption, citified model who never knew the Living Skies
     above Maidstone, Saskatchewan,
                                             the license plate motto come to life.

          in Cold Lake I save money, take my license test with a new used
     beat-up pickup truck, think my way East
                                   to you,   think West
                                   at you
                                             getting there slower

than Greyhound Canada eternity
                                        (a locomotive process

begun in mind, not diesel

) but getting there.

no borders

the farther you can see, the further you want to go.
in the Trizac building, Portage and Main
in the 19th floor staff room
black leather chairs emit
charged sun, heat and hot scent,
city lights slow from the sky down
by stars rising first where windows should be.

I can see clear across the city, the prairie,
the Ontario border   ride highway with eyes
where the blur of trees unsmooths
to rough edges of pine
and big rocks poke like armour
from the stegosaurus shoulders of the road,

rough wings and sharp spines that land evolves
to become a different creature,
one that swallows you
and holds you where I see you

in a Byward gallery: you frame paintings,
listen to Miles Davis   trumpet leads you
colour to colour, rings your eyes
in the closest-corresponding shades of sound

and at the solo, blare of lips' red
and then blush   as when the kiss
of your gaze touched down
and we spoke softly

of when I would leave you,
soft enough
our hearts couldn't hear

ship and bottle

for my brief husband

we walk all night around
the downtown core   turn
about it, within it
ride streets on wasted time.
            carousel
and music of it
slurred by motion
stays in our ears
wherever we go

water
    swung in a pail.

your words drop into it

  one

            by

  one

each splash,   ripple,
    my face   lines of smile

and outside the Windsor Hotel
you tell me a story
about John Candy
on a Harley

                        I remember reading
the Angels are in town
but

under dark folded wings
of city sky, a sense of protection.

we keep walking, pass Pat Friesen scenes
and Big Dave's Big Blues, big as the city
when you walk with no direction,

follow each other, neither leading,
both uncertain.

music gets louder
            at the end of the ride,
coloured lights blur
wonder to confusion.

eyes keep turning as horses slow, stop.
our mothers, across the city,
wait to collect us

                        and we're led away
by responsibility,
back to strange second childhoods
of living-at-home adulthood,

small water of nightlight and sound
            pooled

at the bottom of your bottle,
in the glass wheel
of my
            mind.

route 79

the bus driver leaves his fourways on
½ way down Kenaston   calm pulse
a heart monitor: his daughter
(in his mind
 in the hospital)
is asleep.

easy to forget his caution lights
when, if he keeps them going,
the pulse
(in his mind
 in the hospital)
will always be.

the righthand wiper
sticks again. rain streaks
rightside vision,
muddles streetsigns,
plugs in trees   electric shiver
slices lampposts
in uneven parts.

who can say it's illusion
just because
posts stay standing,
trees don't blow a fuse,
fares aren't getting lost.

she was born so small,
the world shrank.
the things in it, malleable.

her tiny skullbones shift
plates underground,
swallow buses whole.

Times Change(d)

for Patrick Friesen

pausing in the doorway
of the blues bar,
stood still by wellspring sound.
bass pulls you in,
sits you down,

buys you a drink
from the brisk blonde waitress
palefaced in yellow stageglow
that mimics

the streetlights outside,
as though city light
must have a source
and here it is.

I found your book at Borealis
and came here to find you.
they say you moved
but here you are,

fourth-dimension patron
smiling faint
by the window,
bobbing your head to Big Dave.

you watch a train pass,
same one that carried you off
to Vancouver.

music for a moment
sustained
as you recall

the acoustics
of Union Station.

dark factory

dusk is manufactured under trees, begins
as shade and spreads outwards   diffused
by spray of branches, only in
the chillin' of the evening   and runoff

tracked in by cars
with black tires. last evening was a witness
weaving through the neighbourhood

of River Heights. the Height is elm:
where the River? A little boy pees in a sewer grate,
turns his freckled face and grins.
I walk out the sun through a doorway suggested

by poplar and slam it behind me.
cheek to the moon, while other dance partners
line-up against the wallclouds. little boy,
bored of grown-up parties
                                        begins to whistle:

wind comes up
    like a curtain,
            a sun,
        an elevator,

sky curtain: paper sun: glass elevator

and I ride a slow conveyor belt
through a wall-less factory
  as glass catches real sun,
        sets paper on fire,

    curtain goes black with smoke

and everything is real again
except the moon: a crescent: the little boy's smile.
night trickles in an iron grate, is absorbed

by treeroots   raw material
for tomorrow's productivity.

St. James

I
under an umbrella
outside the iron café,
River and Osborne.

kitty corner,
streetkids make deals
at the Centre.

a bus curbs up,
riders fade into fog,
blur of neon signs.

barely caught it,
brief rainbow reflected
on a rainstreaked sky

but I caught it:
cold drop of water
in open palm.

II
slight quiver:
a compass needle
when you look at it.

world for a moment
turns too fast,
centrifuge pulls
whatever together
apart.

III
    I lean

against a wall
on Portage,

    you lean

against a wall
on Rideau.

in the moment
we think of each other,
it is the same wall.

Grant Avenue

Winnipeg under fog,
synchronicity
of cold and dewpoint.

trees assume the velvet
of deer antlers.

a season passes
overnight.

by morning,
the cold hard
world again.

in Assiniboine Forest,
oak trees butt heads,

shyly mate
under slow-falling snow.

prairie girl

only the proud prairie girl
wears plaid in Ottawa,
risks the hick pigeonhole

to wear checkerboard view
from a hang-glider,
truck-launched to Lake Winnipeg
in her West eye.

aluminum wing
the mote that flashes

as she walks downstreet,
lengthens her stride

to catch a thermal.

Kinosoo teeth

Near French Bay, a huge fish leaped from the water,
grasped the canoe into its cavernous mouth,
and snapped it in two.

~ Unattributed,
Treasured Scales of the Kinosoo
Cold Lake Historical Society

Cold Lake karaoke bar

I dedicate this song
to the man I met 5 minutes ago
I dedicate this lung
to a bar full of blue smoke
I dedicate this liver
to the chronic wasting of beer
I dedicate this tube top
to breasts that would hold it up
I dedicate these teeth
to dentistry I couldn't buy them
I dedicate this nervous
to nerves of steel it cleverly conceals
I dedicate me   you   they
couple in cowboy gear   mullet with his own
CD   this music this bar the land it sits on
this whole façade of trying to be
good voices, known lyrics, unseedy
bar, ungreedy owner smiling doing rounds
I dedicate every single thing attempting what
it isn't to the obscure what it is
because the is feels left out
and forgotten, the handyman in the
computer tech the mute in the crooner the
shivering mess in the cool tie the
jackass in the niceguy the
child amassing marbles in the barkeep the
rock chick in the Dixie and the who am I
in the who I am not, pushed
under the surface by all other surfaces
and the playground instructor among
these structures saying don't tell me who
started it so that we'll try

'paralyzers'

because to get drunk on them
has calcium overdose enough
to firm up the skeleton, you could
peel away from flesh,
leave both intact

without bones, not much good
on the dance floor,
only decoration, undecorative,
a failure at what I'm reduced to

'til your brief accidental touch
props me up   yearning core of me
telescopes 'til it hits solid table
and levers me in place,
spokes of irises turn you

while a Halloween monster drinks,
set free   bones on brass tacks
stiffly pivot a new dance craze
we avert eyes from,

us two puddles cupped high
on the worn-in of bar chairs,
waiting to be sat on.

Starz Niteclub

I
tonight, Ripped T-Shirt
warns you away
from his very pregnant girlfriend,

the waitress tries to dust a light
and smashes its cover,
adding sandtraps to 8-Ball,

Geoff the Owner,
not verbally inclined,
makes weird physical jokes,
stack of empty beer mugs
a pile of live grenades.

II
tonight, Ripped T-Shirt
bares his chest,
loyalty strong in him as confusion,

brightness attacks our boredom,
a weak terrorist plot
against comfort

Geoff the Owner
knows a strongman's humour
must be entertained, so we laugh

his meaty hand on your head,
my tiny fingers calming yours.

III
tonight, Ripped T-Shirt
bares his chest,
loyalty strong in him as confusion,
warns you away
from his very pregnant girlfriend,

the waitress tries to dust a light
and smashes its cover,
brightness attacks our boredom,
a weak terrorist plot
against comfort
adding sandtraps to 8-Ball,

Geoff the Owner,
not verbally inclined,
knows a strongman's humour
must be entertained, so we laugh,
make weird physical jokes,

stack of empty beer mugs
his meaty hand on your head,
my tiny fingers calming yours
a pile of live grenades.

signage

quarter after April, cold wind
winds a nothing nowhere town around
a nothing nowhere lake it's named for,

deserted bar afternoon hung with obsolete metal signs
directs attention to no-longer products
as round my wrist and neck, beads lend colour

to false advertisements of utility and
profile   quiet spreading infamy word-of-mouths away
job prospects, no scarlet letter

but forehead billboard
embellished with rumour slogans:

"girl too drunk cheapnight
of the old man two-step"

"weird drug eyes
the Bed & Breakfast café evening"

"two-boyfriends-not-spaced-enough elle"

"one-time Mark's Pub jam guitar chick"

"five jobs in a year Girl Everywhere"

"giggler in public washrooms"

"uncombed morning hair
too-confident heel clack
right through *gasp!* public afterlunch"

"Dad smalltown-famous squadron chief
must cringe and wonder"

so not really here   dull signage me
locomoting, avoiding buyers
through the sparse marina boardwalk midway
of ongoing nothing celebration, nowhere town.

how to smile

for Steve

even pain couldn't drill along byways of nerve fibre
the memory of how you broke each finger
so what you ate for supper from a can in a hurry
is out of the question. what can make you remember, if pain can't,

a thing about me to keep in a zipper pocket of your
motorcycle jacket, shiny pulls reflecting one a.m. Tim Horton's
so that later, when I'm gone from those brief distorted miniatures
you'll inevitably unzip to see what's there

and like a lottery ticket you'd forgotten to check,
a bubblegum comic scented with what memory can't taste,
a number whose song you'd neglected to compose,
an area codename for a girl that lost you,

I'll vaguely appear, inkling that wrinkles your brow
pensive for a word made up to describe it, *sclower,*
trying to make you grin it off your poor, unhappy face
that can't even remember

how to smile

night flying II

for Dizzy

latenight fighter jet engine flush
like heavy traffic a few streets away
half flies / half drives me back to
a studio apartment over Bank Street four years
ago   North Alberta air missing car exhaust
mixed with Nag Champa incense, green pea curry.
cold enough, by open PMQ window

to be sitting in the black plastic chair
on David's balcony, dim-lit Base strains the eyes
like staring in a busier dark, observing night lives
passing solitary down streetlit streets.
some cross to the lighter side to be safe,
others draw to shadows   moths in negative
staying unseen to predators: lascivious pricks,
violent drunks and other wild.

in early morning hours, garbage day scavengers
stop before a pile of putrid treasure,
feel eyes on them but can't find me.
in city night, you feel eyes whether or not they're there.
jets pound away at the sound barrier, drown
certain lyrics, TV lines, soft words a lover says
too shy to repeat, interrupt thoughts.
4 Wing streets go empty as Rockcliffe Base,
the Ottawa downtown 11th floor view

slams down nine stories, crushes innocent dogs
and their walkers, hapless donair eaters and viperish
tokers, crashes me back to Cold Lake.

no one to watch outside, I'm forced to watch
in, notice things about my parents I hadn't.
miss the redheaded poet with the bird's-eye view

until the sandman flies overhead in his F-18,
drops his slow-falling, smoking cargo
to drift in eyes and make me dream speed,
a rapid return.

Kinosoo teeth

displaced urbanite walks innocently
past the Cold Lake North trailer park.
small town sticks you in the teeth of its broken fences, chews/
sucks you in the mouths of its woody knots, swallows/
your disembodied voice sizzles through intestines of phone cord,
feedback buzz digests words to malnourish ears.

it's thirsty in here, dry wires scratch your throat:
hold bottle to baleen maw of landline, strain hops like krill
to nourish a bobbing swim through bluish static.
drowning in want to leave   leaves much for want.
hopeful toes freeze off, unbalance you in the rest of the drink.

Kinosoo Beach is busy in August. in June, you'd hypotherm—
beast get you in its cavernous maw and shut the lights.
frigid springs feed the lake from below,
aquifers pour the best Canadian tapwater
into the café soup kettle, angry broth simmers.
dead-end job lives up to its name.

the day before her coma, the donair slinger's wife
heard her tailings tumour gurgle.
as their daughter and I wiped tables,
Bruce reassured her
it was just the harmonic hum
of industrial fridges,
early morning in a one-mall-town.

Kinosoo, the monster fish
spares none who dare to cross its lake.
not even the motherless five-year-old girl
who summons Bloody Mary daily
in the public restroom,
walks around the mall
for weeks, holding her spectral hand.

escape from Cold Lake

The maiden never saw her brave hunter again, but pieces of the canoe were found floating in the lake the next day. For many years later, no one dared to cross Cold Lake.

~ Unattributed,
Treasured Scales of the Kinosoo
Cold Lake Historical Society

and if we kissed now, would be

sun's rays bracket enough to encaption
a summerful of bright words if closer   this far,
only an excited, non-descript disclaimer

my head throws out spherical auras
tainted with blood-hot byproducts of thought

the earth's grains of dirt rounded
by creature footsteps grain
where circular shadows pioneer

my heart radiates ribs each
with sliding down and off them
gold rings of vital protection, wellbeing

fingerprint whirl windmills
process touch, mill out sensations
to the general countryside

your blue depthless hole-mouth
bottomless of words I haven't heard yet
stretches out-of-whack

and breaks these cycles, all else
the wheeled world over
finds and plies mine

out of round, strips threads,
screw slides out,
bolts pop saying bang:

such tilt-headed doings beyond
the circular reasons
of every single thing else
make sure of nothing

but that the redundant shape
of the world changes slightly

with the gradual feel-good warp
of its finer details.

perspectives

more time spent looking away from each other
than towards, with the car window straight-ahead

or static gaze at different-placed bar TVs,
people-watching on swiveled stools,

then edge of the cold beach midnight:
we try to hold each other still

but shimmering bands of colour
work inside us, unsettle our calm.

when twilight overtakes us we shift into evening.
darkness grows in direct relation to our state.

we own night in a town that sleeps early.

love in wartime

Iraq War, March 2003

in the nightpark under full moon,
over snow packed by the footprints of children,
light from above and below meet in your face:
you are two-dimensional.

outside Iraq the troops are landing.
I ask you to make it stop, and you do;
as god in a dream tends to comply,
you do, but you've only made me forget:

love in wartime
is imperfect,
no longer solves all.

first love rejoices
for the world,
yet I know:

guns are being loaded
in the backs of army trucks
while the road bumps with jolt

of tomorrow's recoil
in parallel time.

startled by the sound
six countries away,
I slip on ice,

grab for the hand
that almost caught me.

the late show

cut eyes on the sun.
visions bleed across the sky

and night falls on the spill,
tangles in hard wires of borealis

that lift it up to an organ-pipe midnight,
pump upside-down hymns,

ring mountain range notation
sung out by staggered lights,

deafening pyrotechnics
choreographed
in a mega-meteor's crater,

soundtrack to a live documentary
explaining the lake's nascence,

sheen of giant glacier
a static smooth as applause.

more of the time

candlelight golds the song
of acoustic guitar,

of the man who holds it
for quick intervals
with his fingers

and more of the time
with his mind.

air above strings
the echo-image of vibrations,

mad blurred tightropes
for a circus

of magnificent
energies

lion and lamb

full-blare moon off a snow lawn needs trimming
basement-windowed underground   cool lair
of helpless creature lain next your reluctant
lion, gold-fringed/

tousled mane that remembers
a hundredth touch by dinner
offers every direction for explanation.

spring lamb never knew the right kind of danger
pink-noses the predator's perked ear, sighs
her biggest small breath   safe nestled in threat,
welcomes the sharp teeth/

senses know safety in his warmth
and scent, reject instinct quiver   slow moon
peels backing off a same-white dawn, confuses
time   could be time for the kill or the chase

but if you choose to hunt
                                        and I refuse to run,
if I let me be caught
                                        and you consume me

then the things nature wants from us are covered.
forget the outside world packed with people who aren't us.
this too is a life, a living:
                                        when we two lie down together,
        their world is over.

irreparable poem

shut into the spare room, white blinds shut–
all I know the whole sky iced into snow
slammed on the ground a dropped book,
no room to walk between sky and ground
or book and floor, all snow or paper now.

white blinds suggest cracks enough to turn pages
or burrow tunnels 'til plows and machines
of de-winter reach our private castle rose midst
parents and authorities too proud to mole
through elements versed better than they
what natural is.

we defy the storm,
carve a snow room,
guard a hard cloud in blizzard–
our frozen clothes shatter,

our bed-warm bodies
bring early spring,

each earthly place
off-limits to love
made irreparably ours

winning streak

global warming North Alberta summer so humid
sugar, salt, parmesan, stick together
so days have more flavour   we get too close

and we stick together. down in your room,
cool damp skin sings warm contact and the top sheet,
Van Morrison sings T.B. Sheets   dust on the needle

crackles him up from basements of vinyl grooves,
iced tea slipstreams slow caffeination, electrifies light
through green Venetian slats   stormclouds skim top

of quiet cottoned in, drag soft subsonic friction
of bath towel: your finegrain cheeks, my latenight legs,
our fog-mirror reflections sharing one skin as

dripping from the shower, drying each other off,
we listen for your parents before we run for it
grab our mixed-up clothes   our one-skin clothes

and streak

escape from Cold Lake

to leave without leaving behind, this time,
lover's weight vs. weight of loss to
carry: the first is lighter

though it pulls fear of uncertainty
like a well-stacked U-Haul trailer.
25 yet pattern-set, three times fled

the untested model grips stomach
like driving too fast downhill, out of mountains
trailing Jasper and Banff as puffs of snow
knock off mud-flaps and drooping bumper,
Cold Lake long since dropped from,

run flat by a highway
of cars   unwitting conspirators.
we don't need a basement room
to change the world outside it
with our thoughts   our last
Provincial Park day, burnt wieners

cold in the middle, devoured hungry
to affirm his hard-won wet wood fire
with human ritual,
we made the back seat
of his Ford station wagon
into a bedroom different

than it had ever been before.
it stayed that way even when
the sun came up empty
on the spot we'd been.
one of these thrift stores
we'll get curtains, but for now

Rockies hang in grey-blue folds
over windows to shield us
from view, muffle the trickle
of ice-fed waterfalls.
leaving behind without leave this time

so his parents would leave him
unfrustrated to pack—
we'll call them tonight from Calgary
with a safe enough distance
of phone wire between us
to circle the Olympic Park
seven hundred times
in a newly-sanctioned event
called Escape from Cold Lake.
hubcaps, the spinning medals

glint gold by sunset
we receive joyfully and tearfully,
CD player skips *O Canada*
preferring Pixies,
our flame flag waves high
from the top of Calgary Tower

and every red maple leaf
Chinook-melted of snow
quivers triumph
against a white winter sky.

this time, to leave without leaving
behind, to leave without leave

is half the watch I'm happy to share
as he asks me again
and I take his right hand
and say, this

is what time it is,
finally,
we waited
so long

what I saw in him: an epilogue

turvy vision of muscular arm,
strong hand ending in bouquet
of apologetic ditch daisies:
whole-body frisson

like hearing philharmonic
the first time,
stoned and blindfolded.

what I heard in him:
a Beethoven piece trembling,
transcendent, *Symphony No. 3*

played by impossible orchestra
of violins, dulcimers, and zithers
in a commodious closet of Alps.

only slum infestation
and floor-mattress poverty,
jealous paranoia
and outrageous blame,

workplace thievery,
gambling addiction,
brief pregnancy
and anguished abandonment:

only the city
could blind the eyes
I had back then.

what I saw in him:
rust-coloured stubble,
tiny lanterns illuminated
by the roric dawn.

Dedicated to my parents Hal and Myrna Fuhr, my brother Jeff Fuhr and family (Laura and Alanna), sorely missed grandparents Walter and Diana Fuhr and Mary Helen Britton, and to best childhood base brat best friends Jennifer MacDonald (CFB Baden-Soellingen, West Germany), Cyndi Bilodeau (CFB / 4 Wing Cold Lake), and Armour Garland (CFB Rockcliffe, Ottawa). Thanks to all who appear in these pages for the inspiration. And to Craig Galambos, my one true love, that these pages should help you know me better.

Full posting dates for fellow brats:
Cold Lake 1981-1985;
Baden-Soellingen 1985-1990;
Cold Lake 1990-1994;
Ottawa 1994-1998;
Winnipeg 1998-2001;
Cold Lake 2001-2004.

acknowledgements

Some poems appeared in present or previous form in the chapbook *the lens of love* (Loft on Eighth 2017), *night flying* (pooka press 2009), in the anthology *evergreen: six new poets* (Black Moss Press 2002), and in publications *THIS Magazine, Freefall, Peter F. Yacht Club* (various issues, above/ground press), *Modomnoc, Bywords, SPIRE, Carleton Arts Review, The Charlatan, This Is Carleton, White Wall Review, It's Still Winter, ottawater 01,* and as an above/ground press broadside (*prairie cryptic*). In a previous form, the manuscript for this book was shortlisted for the Robert Kroetsch Prize for Innovative Poetry from *Matrix Magazine* in 2016, judged by George Elliott Clarke.

Poems from this book were graciously featured on a CJSW (University of Calgary) campus radio podcast called *Notes from the Underground Three* by Victoria Stanford in 2016, re-circulated in part by pearl pirie on *Literary Landscapes* at CHUO (University of Ottawa) radio in Ottawa.

Some poems received editing advice from generous souls including George Amabile (Writer in Residence, Winnipeg Public Library, 2000), Stuart Ross (Cobourg), Richard Harrison (Calgary), Joanna Drummond (Calgary), and fellow members of Ottawa's Peter F. Yacht Club writing workshop collective (particularly rob mclennan, Stephen Brockwell, pearl pirie, Brian Pirie, Vivian Vavassis, and jwcurry), and of course Micheline Maylor and Neil Petrunia of Frontenac House.

The Carolyn Forché line in "field recording" (page 27) is from "all the way to the end" from her collection *Blue Hour.*

Thank you Canada Council for the Arts, Calgary Arts Development, and The Banff Centre for the Arts for the opportunity to participate in Writing Studio 2016 and polish poems with editing suggestions from Karen Solie, Lisa Robertson, and Michael Dickman. Lauren Carter provided feedback on some work as Writer in Residence at the Alexandra Writers' Centre in Calgary, 2015. Profound gratitude to Dave Eso of Migratory Words and Canmore's artsPeak Festival for the opportunity to participate as a festival writer-in-residence along with Robert Kroetsch, Chris Masson, and Tim Murphy in 2011, and for their feedback on this work.

biography

Laurie Fuhr's writing has been published in anthologies such as *Rogue Stimulus: The Stephen Harper Holiday Anthology for a Prorogued Parliament* (Mansfield Press 2010), *Leonard Cohen: You're Our Man* (Foundation for Public Poetry Montreal, 2009), and in periodicals in Canada and abroad like *THIS Magazine, White Wall Review, Carleton Arts Review, Nod Magazine, Go! Magazine* (San Francisco), *Journal of Literature & Aesthetics* (India), and *FreeFall.*

An air force brat, she used to live in Germany, Cold Lake, Ottawa, and Winnipeg, but has lived in Calgary since 2004, serving as Managing Editor for *filling Station* magazine from 2008-2011 and now as a poetry instructor at the Alexandra Writers' Centre Society and host of the Single Onion Open Mic. Connect on Facebook at @MultimodalPoet. She is also a musician; have a listen at birdheatmusic.com.